ACKNOWLEDMENTS

Branding Basics 1.0 was in the making for quite some time now and over this time there are a lot of people who have contributed in the completion of the book either directly or indirectly.

I would like to thank all the brands that me and my company Brand Protocol have worked with in the past and even today.

I would like to thank my mother Meena Pillai, my sister Jaishree Pillai and my best friend Aryan Chaudhary without whom this book wouldn't have been completed.

ABOUT THE AUTHOR

Chetan Pillai is a Brand Marketer, Socialpreneur, Mentor, Investor & Traveller. He loves to work with people who see problems as an opportunity to excel and grow in life. After spending more than 9 years building, designing and marketing brands and after having opportunities to work with some of the finest brands today like The Times Of India, Monsanto India, Fitness First, Bharat Matrimony.com, IndiaProperty.com and many more and helped them achieve their marketing and branding goals, he realised that there is a huge gap between what organizations think about their brands and how they market it.

He realised that there was a desperate need to create awareness and fill gaps where businesses fail to understand the impact of branding in the marketing process. The problem was not in doing it, because everybody is doing it and everybody is broadcasting information; but it was about how to do it right? His only goal right now is to help businesses all over the world achieve their marketing and branding goals faster and in an easier way.

He is already helping many brands from big corporates to startups to achieve their marketing and branding goals with his company Brand Protocol, which is into strategic brand development and marketing through digital media.

One important lesson that he wants to share from his experience is, "Don't communicate until you know exactly who you are and why you matter. Only then you are ready to share your message with the world."

Index

Introduction

Chapter 1: Defining a Brand
What is a Brand?
How a brand is defined in the digital world?

Chapter 2: **Phases of Brand Development**
Brand Research
Brand Platform
Brand Architecture
Brand Naming
Visual Expression
Brand Execution
Brand Alignment
Clearing Misconceptions

Chapter 3: Fabricating Brand Strategy
Consistency is the Key
Key Ingredients for Building a Great Brand
Brand Value Proposition
Building Buyer Personas

Chapter 4: Putting your Brand into Action
How to use Buyer Persona
How to build a Brand Experience
Great Brand = Great Content + Wow Experience
Importance of Social Media
Identifying a Brands Voice
Presentation & Appearance

Chapter 5: Monitoring your Brand
Brand Observation
Managing the Bad
Celebrating the Good

Chapter 6: Measuring Your Brand
Measuring the ROI

Conclusion

Introduction

If you're a marketer or an entrepreneur, you might have noticed that a lot of things about the subject of branding have changed over the last decade. How you brand your business is no longer just a matter of implementing clever, creative, and timely ad placements.

Focus should be on converting strangers into visitors and convert visitors into leads and leads into customers and then convert the customers into brand advocates.

Now let's talk about the first step of the inbound marketing technique, for example: getting found by potential customers. Now days a business is one of the billions of results on the Google search results. And if it's not one of the ones on the first page, they're essentially lost. A building's super sweet sign is just one of the thousands of visual ad's bombarding overstimulated passers-by every day. And the promotional giveaway that once tickled entrants' fancies? Now it looks like nothing more than a spammy banner ad.

Making a brand stand out and appear trustworthy to the right audience is, needless to say, no piece of cake. Successfully managing your brand in the inbound age is about more than just connecting all the phases of the marketing funnel and creating content that attracts and converts leads. It's about doing all of that.

It's a tricky thing to get right, because branding encapsulates anything you do that contributes to your customers' opinions and feelings about your company.

Ultimately, the key is making "branding" into a measurable metric for which you can show concrete results.

This book will show you exactly how to do that in an inbound framework and create effective, recognizable brands in the digital age.

Chapter – 1
Defining a Brand

What is a Brand? Who needs one? Where does it live? How do I start? Can anybody do it? Can you start at any time? Well the interesting thing is it's what gets you up in the morning, it's the thing that is the pile of light that fuels your passion, it's the thing that the world would miss if you weren't here, it is your magnetic north.

So having a brand is a really important part of being a small business it is going to help you distinguish yourself from others. It's going to help you stake out your territory in the world, help you understand your audience and your connection to them and it's going be the thing that makes the whole greater than the sum of the parts.

So where does your brand live exactly, is it your logo, your business cards, your signage, your flyers or your radio advertising campaign that you do well. Well these are all maybe manifestations of your brand but your brand largely lives in the hearts, minds and souls of your employees and your customers. You and your team are what holds the brand and it's shared by your customers in their hearts and souls and minds, it doesn't live anywhere else.

You can't point to it and say that's a brand that's been manufactured because it lives in the hearts and souls and minds of everybody involved. It's really important to start thinking about how that is going to fuel the choices you make as far as your behaviour is concerned. How you take returns, how you bake your recipes, the methods that you use, the processes that you deploy, those will all be part of your secret sauce that go into what your brand is.

Building a business is really hard, and people think that they know what's best for you. Everybody in your life, your family, your neighbours and co-workers they are all going to tell you how you're supposed to run your business but the truth is that nobody knows what's best for you.

Your only responsibility is to put the time and the energy, to learn what it is that you're trying to do well enough that you're not leaving anything to chance. So if you are hoping to learn about brand that means that you are already driven, you are already asking questions, you are saying I don't know everything and I'm going to turn to a resource that might help me get there. In every facet of your business whether it comes to your finances, your hiring practices or your legal utilities give yourself that opportunity to think about your business in a dynamic way and as someone who has been fortunate enough to advise hundreds of venture-backed startups or the world's largest corporations; I am telling you none of them have the secret recipe. They don't know how to do this better or faster than you. They simply take the time to ask the questions and that's what I ask you to do, ask yourself those open ended questions, get a lay of the land and get it to a place where you don't have to reference a book, you don't have to turn to your notes but you just get it.

You can explain it to your spouse, you can talk about it with your neighbours, and you have no problem standing in front of a camera describing the topic when you get to that place. You will arrive at an understanding that will ensure the health and well-being of your business so that when you do wrap it in a brand you're proud of all of it. You are not just proud of the storefront, you're not just proud of that employee or that product, you are proud of everything that you've built.

In the digital marketing age, branding refers to branding on the internet – and the internet is very fast and dynamic. Brands can be built and destroyed just as quickly.

"Overnight success," although tempting, is not a good goal for a brand to have. A successful brand should be built up over time. A slow, gradual build-up provides the opportunity to reach far more people than some flash-in-the-pan fad that's here today and gone tomorrow. (Although, keep in mind that if you're not careful, even a slowly built-up brand can still fall in an instant.)

The internet is the great equalizer, giving small companies the potential to have a big voice.

But to get to the point where your voice is big, you not only need to be good at getting found – you need to have a differentiator

How a brand is defined in the digital world?

If a brand is able to find out its uniqueness or its differentiator then it becomes its calling card. It's how everyone recognizes them and the first thing everyone judges them by. So it needs to be consistent. No matter which channels your customers choose to interact with your brand – your website, blog, email, Facebook, Twitter, or whatever tomorrow's technology may bring – they should all demonstrate the unique experience that your brand represents.

For example, if we talk about Southwest airlines they are not the best airlines in the world nor they the most cheapest but what they deliver to their customers is an experience of being in the south west airline plane. One of the experiences I recall is when I reached my seat on the plane and opened the luggage flap to keep my bag there was a flight attendant right inside the luggage compartment to welcome me on the flight. This was an experience I never had with any of the airlines I travelled so far and whenever next Southwest Airline plane I look forward to the surprises I might get and the brand experience.

If you notice all of Southwest Airlines branding and marketing communication, from their flights to their social media, is designed around that basic premise and it remains consistent throughout the company's marketing. When creating your own branding, you should strive for that same consistency. Visually, a brand should include the same elements across all channels, such as logo, color, fonts, tone and the way the brand message is communicated. But design consistency is just the first step. The most important thing is to set expectations for the experience that customers will have every single time they interact with your brand online. It should transcend each channel (and even the internet itself) to be instantly recognizable as yours.

Chapter 2
Phases of Brand Development

Brand Research

One of the major requirements in any brand development process is research I know that sounds familiar and we all quote do research whenever we get the chance but if you're going to be building a brand which is trying to create a connection with an audience then the research has to be very different.

A normal research would include things like knowing who your customer is but let's go beyond that right. Now let's think about this psyche we're trying to create so if you know what you're great at making or you know what service you're great at providing don't just think about it in its own venue because you are too close to it you are the maker of it your employees your advisers they are too close to it you need to distance yourself you need to learn more about the customers lifestyles and interests and ways of thinking so that you can directly relate to the way that they're contemplating your product or service.

So when I say brand research perfect example is I know you research your competitors what about your indirect competitors when I say indirect that means not someone selling the same thing to the same customer but selling an alternative right if I ask you about a yogurt shop so you're launching a yogurt shop your direct competitors or of course anyone who's also selling yogurt and you might say to me well maybe ice cream shops as well but if you break down what yogurt or ice cream is it's a three dollar treat that gives you five minutes of happiness okay well what are the three dollar treats bring you five dollars of happiness you can learn a lot about what your customer needs emotionally just by considering who has a like-minded business model but sell something completely different so when you're thinking about brand research you're focusing on the emotional connection between you and your customer.

Don't make a decision for them empathize, contemplate, consider the way that they're thinking about things and figure out what lifestyle experience they hope to have with your brand present and you can learn so much again not just from your direct competitors from your indirect competitors as well.

Another key component in brand research is that any brand lives in the hands of employees, right? You might be the CEO or founder of your business but; are you going to be on the street every day? Are you going to be in all the sales calls for the life of your business? Definitely not so who are speaking on behalf of you are they your employees or your analysts or your investors whoever they might be you have to ensure that you're not only creating a language for your customer you're creating a language for the employees to ensure that when they promote the story it aligns exactly with your business's promise that's why you also have to do research into the type of people that work in your business, the type of people who are going to come to this place and serve your promise so it's very important to know them well otherwise you'll never be able to create a brand program that will deliver on your brand promise.

Brand Platform

So in the earlier section I referenced the notion of the words in a brand right there are visuals and then there are words. When you talk about words there's also a way to package them, so many of us have heard of things like a mission statement right? We've heard about them our whole lives but do we really understand what they are? Well I would say in a brand context a mission statement is a description of what you do as functionally as possible no sex appeal to it. You don't have to be over dynamic a functional description of what you do. Spend some time creating your mission statement because that's a hard thing to create.

Now if you've got that mission statement the next ingredient should probably be something like a vision statement and I like to say that vision is short for visionary right? that means big and audacious and beyond what can be measured right? Now if you look up what Nike or Apple promises in their vision statement you see there's no measurement, they don't say I'm going to sell X number of shoes or provide this type of customer service they're talking about intangible goals. You've got your mission statement as that foundation and as I told you it has to be really functional but the vision statement is supposed to be big and emotional.

Great! now you're starting to build a framework for all the words to populate. No you have got your functional words, you have got your audacious words and the words in the center are called "brand positioning". The place, the position in the market that's exclusively yours to claim and you don't sound like someone else here or walk like someone else or work like someone else but you have your own unique position in the market. For example: If we have to talk about cars there are thousands of car makers right, a lot of them. Ok so how about luxury cars? How about European luxury cars? How about European luxury sports sedans? You get that I just eliminated all the other conversation pieces and we're only talking about specifically the position in the market that those automobile manufacturers are trying to hone. You too have to do this in your business, you cannot be all things to all people.

So if you functionally describe your mission and you talk about your audacious big objective for the category and what you hope is going to happen to the world because you exist and then you fill it with the positioning, well this is how I describe the place that we call "home"

Now you have context, now you have vocabulary that can absolutely inform how you train your employees, how you give a speech, how you write marketing vocabulary, a couple of two other components that are timely and relevant are what we call "brand personality" and "brand pillars"

For example: Get on a Southwest flight and its the same plane as any other company could fly, same airports but for some reason being on Southwest feels different why because the way in which they carry themselves and their brand persona it is their personality.

Pick any brand in your life Coca-Cola, Pepsi, Ford it doesn't matter you can create a human character, in the same way you can draw your own character for your business. Decide how you want to carry yourself? How you're going to make people feel when they're in your presence that's the personality.

Let's talk about "Brand Pillars". Pillars are the foundation, let's just say that you're a really ethical business and you might be selling shoes to the masses but ethically that is a foundation. Your mission is going to be built on that foundation then your position and then your vision, now also decide what are the things you're always going to stand for no matter how the market evolves. Now if you've got your pillars, mission, positioning and vision now you wrap it in your personality and then you will have context, vocabulary and understanding and these are the things that make a brand strong.

Brand Architecture

Earlier we've talked about things like the words that you use to describe your business but you have to respect that you might have a business name and you might have a portfolio of services but you might actually name them like you might actually decide that it's not just one company, its like having multiple companies under one.

Lets take example of what Apple does, they don't just say everything is Apple but there's Apple and then they have the iPhone product line which has multiple variations or the iPod which has been around a long time with hundreds of iterations, colors and shapes now because they've got a master brand called Apple and a sub brand called iPod and then they have multiple versions of it, this makes it very easy for you and I to have this conversation. It's science, its that architectural structure that defines how these products and services are related to one another is actually called "Brand Architecture".

It's the way in which you manage what products and services you provide so it makes it as easy as possible for people to understand. Like it's not about what Microsoft Word or Microsoft Photoshop it's about Microsoft Office likewise it's not about Adobe Photoshop, Adobe Illustrator and Adobe InDesign but it's about Adobe Creative Suite. It simplifies the related products and services so that consumers can build a relationship with multiple things at the same time.

Brand Architecture is simply the mapping of what your intentions are? How many products and services are you going to offer? How are they related to one another? And, How they are not related?

For example: BMW owns Mini Cooper they intentionally keep them separate because the Mini Cooper owner wants to drive a Mini and the BMW owner wants to drive BMWs. If you even look at the BMW's brand architecture you'll notice that it's not just BMW, there's the three series the five series the seven series and will see how they've created like an alphanumeric system to make it as easy as possible for you to understand what model is right for you, how to upgrade and how do you represent your personal character. If I am sporty and young I'm going to drive a 3-series, you get that context while that framing of those products and services makes them easier for people to find, buy and then ultimately advocate for like literally explain it to their friends and say I bought the m5 because……. and that makes people more proud of their associations and they tend to upgrade faster.

So again we call that brand architecture the way in which you manage your portfolio of brand assets so that they feel related to one another so that consumers can make the easiest choice possible, be proud of what they've chosen and know exactly how to sustain their relationship with your brand.

Naming

If you noticed I didn't start with naming but most people start with naming because they think that they could come up with a business idea and name it immediately and start doing business. But before you do that you have to respect that "Naming" is an incredibly daunting task. I don't know anybody who is actually that great at coming up with a name in an instant, this means that there must be a process to building a name. In fact you have to ask yourself what you ultimately intend to do with the name because there's no such thing as a cool name. I'm sorry but I've never seen one and I don't recollect any example of a known brand with a cool name.

For example, is Coca-Cola a great name coca is an affiliation with cocaine which used to be a core ingredient in Cola. Now is that a good name? Or how about Google you don't even know what a Google is? It sounds like a baby babbling doesn't it? But a Googolplex is the number one followed by a hundred zeros a large number representing all the data that Google is sorting through. Okay, lets take one more example of "Nike" do you want a name like Nike? It's mispronounced in most countries around the world most people say "Naik". You see that you have this affiliation with what you think a good name is and unfortunately you're biased.

Based on the experience you have with a brand because of the relationship its shares with you. The kind of relationship Starbucks or Ferrari has shares with you, do you think that the name is good the answer is NO but in the truth you actually are just using it as a reference point. So when you think about a name the intention should be to make it a trigger, it's just a starting point of a relationship. Hopefully people will say the name, hear the name, be able to pronounce the name and then it just triggers a whole bunch of affiliations. So like I gave you example of Nike and you probably went off into this distant land you started thinking of athletes and uniforms and shoes and you probably must have went all over the place with it because they've taken their name and they've affiliated with a lot of things.

These are the things that you as a target consumer love so when you're trying to pick a name you really have to decide what you want it to represent more than anything and there's a process to go through and I will make it really quick and simple for you.

I just described you that you have to decide what position in the market you intend to claim with this name. Literally what place are we going to call home? Once you've studied that well now you should know about who are all the competitors, what are their names like, are they long or are they short, are they funny or are they colourful. Just get a sense of those organizations so you don't come up with a name that sounds similar. And then once you've done that you have to go through a series of brainstorming processes.

Now the brainstorming process works like this, you basically have to tell yourself there's not such thing as a wrong name because the name process requires up to about a thousand names to find the best one. So that means you got to have to let yourself go because then you don't get to say, "that's a stupid name" or "that name doesn't work for these nine reasons". Instead, you just want to get the ideation process started and the best way to start is to write a five-word sentence that describes your
business, not even a sentence just give me five words.

Let's take Amazon Kindle, let's just say that we were going to name that together. First we have to ask ourselves, what's the position in the market that we're trying to claim? So go ahead and do that for yourself. Great what are the names of all the competitive devices? Okay, just put it all on the wall don't try to remember it, just put it on the wall. Now you know what names are distracting you, what names people say most often, why do they say it most often etc and now you're going to get into a place where you're going to describe the function of the Amazon Kindle. Maybe the function is how the screen works, maybe it's how easy it is to port information on and off of it or whatever those descriptions are give yourself those words and this is where the ideation really comes in.

Once you've picked a word let your mind wander think about all the things that you affiliate with that word so if the word was portable with Kindle. Now let anybody in the room screen one word out please say a word but not portable. It can be like small, light, easy to pack etc., just let yourself wander let all of those concepts come out of your consciousness and do not constrain yourself. Don't say "NO" don't say "BAD" just get them all out and you'll notice what starts to happen here is you start to back away from your products function and concentrate more into the effect that it's going to have on peoples life, how they're going to feel about your product or service. So as you go about that process think about it we just picked five words or so but you can create a long list of concepts and now you get to play, pick a match. In this process lets say you have decided that I'm going to come up with a word which means this device is supposed to get people to imagine and read and think creatively. I want to ignite their understanding because reading is about ignition of consciousness and I know we're going to Kindle, we're going to Kindle their thoughts through content consumption on this magnificent device that's why we should call it the "Amazon Kindle".

Let yourself go through that process and only then will you arrive at a destination. I request do not land without at least ten names because half of them are going to get booted as soon as you start searching the internet or visit the Patent and Trademark websites. You can conduct a search and find out if there's a trademark already in place for the name that you've just created go to Google or any search engine and type in those terms and see who else is using that vocabulary and eventually you'll get down to a minimum of three names.

Eventually when you decide on a name you have to file for a trademark and there's tons of ways to go about it. Do not use them until you have gotten permission back from your legal because whatever you think you're trying to grow with your business, one trademark infringement will put you out of business. That's why it's so important to go through that competitive research, it's so important to think about what you're trying to accomplish, so important to think about all the words that you would affiliate so that when you pick that name you believe in it. When you try to register the domain secure the trademark and eventually promote it to the market. You don't have anything to worry about you know that it's right and now you can focus on your business.

Visual Expression

At this point we've talked about a lot of things, we've talked about how you decide on the way you're going to manage your portfolio of products and services that's called brand architecture. We've also talked about naming what you're going to call something, we've talked about the research that's necessary to make any of these types of recommendations. Well along with all of those components of course comes the visual language. In fact you saw branding and you said logos in your consciousness but nobody ever bought anything because a logo is pretty but what the logo again does much like a name is it provides a trigger point or recall, it's supposed to invite the consumer into a new place so that they think about your business.

Well if the logo is just the introduction what's the rest of the visual experience? Here comes a series of really simple components so if you think about a logo it not only has the words but often has shapes. So brands have a series of shapes, think about any organization you can think of like the Coca-Cola logo as an example it's the swirly shape, it's not just the words or the bottle cap or the shape of the bottle. Great brands have shapes affiliated with them, how about the color red synonymous with that institution. If I say green you might say John Deere, if I say brown you say UPS, say purple and orange you say FedEx. So great brands also play claim to a color now you can't have exclusive rights to a color but you can absolutely pick a color that no one in your category has ever used.

Another component are the photos that you use to portray your business, the customer experience whatever that might be and please don't leave your photos to chance. Don't just pick some random ones or borrow some from friends if you recognize that the brands that you admire most honestly the ones you feel the strongest connection to their photography directly relates to the brand experience. You tend to have right the photos, have the right lighting, the right characters, the right dress all of the things that constitute the image experience. We've talked about things like the colors, the shapes, the words in the letter form which is typography or fonts, now you can start to see how all these things come together.

You can take any brand that you know and love and you'll recognize that there absolutely is a visual vocabulary, a way in which they're communicating to you with a whole series of visual experiences what we call that "Visual Expression". The way in which you are expressing your brand visually and it's imperative that you don't stop at the logo because when I start reading your brochure, swimming through your website, going to your tradeshow is it going to stop with the logo or am I going to see an integrated visual experience where a select few colors, the right lighting and the right type of photographs all of these shapes intertwined together to create a synchronized experience that we call visual expression.

Brand Alignment

If you pick up any business theory book or any magazine that's telling you how to grow your organization everyone will tell you that got to focus on the employees, so I don't think this is going to be some new information for you but what's really important about the employee base is not just that they know how to do their job or they know what they're being measured on but what matters really is that they believe that they actually believe in what it is that you are trying to share with them.

For example when you think about a faith, it's not just about the symbol of the faith or it's not just about the books that tell the stories of the faith but it's all about the believers of faith. Whether it's the religious leader or the constituents they all are aligned, they all understand how this should matter and how its affect the way that they carry themselves.

Every organization with either one employee or a thousand employees has to ensure that the employee base the voice of the business are all aligned around the brand and what it believes and what makes it different. No let's take the Salesforce as a perfect example, now most sales forces are trained on how the utility works, here's what we sell and this is how it functionally works or they're really good at negotiation but what happens when you go into a business meeting and the sales deal is almost done and the clients potential client says "Well, what makes you guys different I know that the software and the hardware but really what is it that you believe?" and if that sales person can't come up with an answer then that says well what is going to happen to that sale.

Now the important question to ask is, What we want the world to know about our brand and what we teach all of our employees and what they stand for. S whenever you're going through this process of constructing your business and then wrapping it in a brain and you cannot stop with the senior executive team because you'll ultimately realize when you get to five employees, 100 employees or a thousand employees that the senior executives are running the business, they're not promoting the business. Maybe they give a speech at a conference but day to day who is on customer service call, whose greeting people at the front door, who's responding with emails, who's writing the brochure copy, those people are your employee base. They represent your brand and you have to ensure that once you have constructed this brand, you've done the research, you have theorized around the name, you have decided what the portfolio is supposed to look like and you have wrapped it in a visual system but don't just leave it in the PowerPoint don't just leave it in brand guidelines that your designer holds but teach every employee about the research you did, teach them about what you learned about the competition, teach them about what you've learned about the consumer, who the buyer is and how they feel, what they believe, where they go and what they do? Doesn't that sound like a recipe for a great high producing employee, off course it does.

I have also found that employees who believe in the organization they are working for actually know how to articulate it. They are more proud of where they work, they tell their family and friends about it more often, they work harder, they work longer why because they are not punching a clock anymore they're not pulling a lever or throwing a dart but they specifically are creating something that goes beyond things and that can be measured.

If you ever go to a store where you feel like the employees really want to be there no whip can ever make an employee love a business but a reason to believe a philosophy, a way of seeing the world but all of these things together. That's what people want that's what a business owes them and that's why it's called brand alignment.

Brand Extension

Now when your business has grown beyond a single brand or a few product brands or a whole system, as we have described earlier, ultimately you are going to get to a place where you are going to want to grow your business and want to offer something new and it might be a derivative of what you've already done. You might acquire somebody who offers a complimentary service and follow the process of strategic brand development. You don't leave those things to chance instead you create a recipe for it and the recipe is referred to as brand extension.

How you decide what is extendable when it comes to your brand. So in order to do this you can't just again make it up but you have to think about it. You have to calculate what you think is really going to happen so you can pick any brand as an analogy. For now I'll just pick something that I think would be relevant to all of you let's take the brand Ford. It's public, people are familiar with it and it's got an international base. If I ask you what business Ford is in? you might say they're in automobiles, I agree they're in automobiles are they also in variations of automobiles like compact to truck. They make a lot of different types of vehicles and you can see that already. The brand is extendable but it doesn't just mean one thing it means a couple things. Ok in this case, where does my relationship with Ford end? Well probably not just at the car but maybe on the key chain, sign in my driveway or on my personal website where I express my affinity for Ford. It can also be in the t-shirt that I wear or my hat or my mobile phone case. I'm just giving a really simple example that the Ford relationship doesn't stop at the vehicle it has a lot of other facets to it and brand extension is the study of all of those sort of slightly connected assets.

These slightly connected opportunities where you say your consumer your relationship doesn't stop here it starts here and it grows off in a series of different directions. Now I know this sounds like a field day and everybody's excited to do these types of things so have fun but remember that if it's not on slightly connected to your brand you're going to damage your brand.

Before making any decision about your brand, ask yourself how it is going to impact your brand even if its about changing the carpet, hiring a new employee, putting some content on the website or giving a speech ask yourself is it on brand, does it align, does it match, does it connect with what my employees think and expect what my customers think and expect what makes us different from the competition.

So when you go through the brand extension process it's actually not hard to create the extensions the priority is constrain them, protect yourself, don't overextend, don't go too far, don't be too drastic because if I take you too far down the road you are going to start to call into question what that organization is doing?

Hypothetically what if we said that Ford was in the restaurant business now you that you you can't even connect that in your consciousness because there is no correlation it's not on-brand right, so ultimately your responsibility is to assess all the components of your brand and how they are connected to the audience and then decide what's extendable and then once you've assessed what's extendable just make sure that you're not compromising the brand equity you've already built because that was hard to construct. Remember it took a lot of efforts to construct those connections so don't overextend them, instead plan for them and verify them before you execute and now you'll have a massive portfolio.

Brand Execution

At this point after you have gone through all the phases of brand development, you recognize there's a process that's why I call it strategic brand development. You can't say let's make a brand overnight instead you need to say let's plan, let's think strategically about what we're trying to construct and ultimately you'll get to some end-user experiences and that's what we call brand execution. The way in which you're executing or putting out the brand depending on whether you are B2B or B2C doesn't matter but you can figure out where the consumer is going to touch your brand. We call those touch points as brand touch points.

Its about everything you do, right from the email you send, the email signature, tone of voice with a customer service help, your brochure that is sent or the sales sheet that is broad or the PowerPoint presentation that's delivered or the web video or the store experience. All of those things are a combination of all the assets we reviewed in the past, the way you name yourself and the way your portfolio services are managed etc. well

When you take the words and the visuals integrate to create your brand experience now you have what an artist would call a pallet. So let's just say you hire someone to build your brochure, now you say go make me a brochure and they have to start from nothing. They have to go write some words, drum up some pictures, start with some art and of course they are going to fail at it the first ten times. It's a hard thing to do but what if you gave them a recipe book as in these are the words we use and this is how we sound different this is what we believe, this is what we hope is going to happen to the world, these are our colors, systems and this is how they are different. This color means this, that color means that, this shape is specifically for that market and now when you hand all of these assets to your brand executors, your graphic designer and your web developer are not in a cloud of confusion anymore because now they actually have all the ingredients they need to construct something that's going to be right probably the first time when you are planning to execute your brand.

Stop and ask yourself who that audience is and how are they going to touch my brand so that I can create brand executions that serve their needs. What are those brand executions made of? Well there's got to be words and there's got to be visuals and those words and visuals come from our brand platform, the place in the market that's ours to claim that mission and vision and tagline. All of those ingredients are how you are going to say what you do, your visual component tree, your photography and colors and shapes etc
are going to be the look in what you do.

When you smash those together to create a web experience or design a vehicle or whatever those touch points are then you are not hoping or you are not pretending or you are not leaving it to chance but what you are really trying to do is being very calculated about the choice. And if this sounds like it's been a long process what about the process of fixing something that you built that's broken. That's way more expensive, spending time to construct something that's bad and then paying the price to fix it later costs way more than just starting from the right place, moving through the right steps and coming to a conclusion that nobody has the right to take from you.

Summary

We are all moving quickly we are all a tight for making a lot of decisions so I just wanted to give you a quick summary of the things that I think are most relevant to an entrepreneur and that is do not build your business starting with your logo or your name because it takes time and energy to construct those things and they're not the starting point, you don't want to just have a child and name it and hope that it's right but you think about it, you try to create a connection and a story behind it.

Same thing with your visual systems, don't pick what colors you like because you are not the customer. Find colors that relate to the consciousness of the decision-maker "the buyer". When it comes to an entrepreneur and their willingness to get out and communicate they honestly always forget about how important it is to make sure that someone isn't already doing what you're doing so instead of doing the work and then seeing start with the research, start with the evaluation of all of the places where your brand is going to manifest itself and simply take record of it. Take photos, tear out articles, make notes or whatever you need to do and make a room in your office. Update it whenever necessary but the more you're aware of what they are doing and saying the better chance you'll have that.

You will never do or say what others or your competition is doing. In the human psyche the hardest thing for us to do is to differentiate and you will notice that when you're walking around you are comparing things constantly; it's just the way that our minds work.

So why not make that easier for your consumers to differentiate your brand from the rest. So if you're an entrepreneur building a business and you want to brand yourself you cannot start at the name and the logo those come multiple phases later. So eventually you have to get to a place where you realize that that brand experience you are creating has to represent something much larger than your institutional philosophy. It's about how you hope to effect the world making those decisions and locking down those components will ensure that as you spend this money and this energy constructing this brand experience you're not leaving anything to chance and that's what an entrepreneur or a leader has to focus on.

Chapter 3:
Fabricating a Brand Strategy

Building a brand strategy is a long-term plan for developing a successful brand presence in order to achieve specific goals.

When you think about what a brand actually equals, honestly it's made up of a whole series of parts but the best way to think about it is that a brand is broken out into words and visuals. So what I want to say "words" which might be the content on a home page or the message on a business card or content on a letterhead or how about the words that the CEO uses at a speech. All of those things are verbal representations of the brand but they don't stand alone. The words that I mentioned in a brochure or on a business card are wrapped in artistry and that's the visual component tree.

Every brand is partially the words that are used partially and the visual system wrapped together to create the experience, something like walking into Starbucks - the signage and the way the products are named are the words that the customer service staff uses and the visuals are the colors, the materials that the tables are made out of now you can write those things together and think about it as to how you can create a unique brand experience for your brand and think about what you're trying to construct or are you just trying to wrap things like a present. Words along with visuals, if you wrap them together now you are creating a brand experience.

Before we start let's erase the biggest myths about brand strategy: your brand is not your product, your logo, your website, or your name. In reality, your brand is far more enveloping — it defines the natural and frequently intangible aspects of your company identity. A well thought out and defined brand identity should be the backbone of any successful company, particularly for online enterprises that typically lack the physical brand components of brick-and-mortar stores. It's that hard-to-pin-down feeling that separates powerhouse and mediocre brands from each other, and a big part of that hard-to-pin-down feeling comes from brand consistency. Let's dig into that a little deeper.

Consistency is the Key

Now lets see what should brand consistency involve? Here are some of the basic elements that should remain the same for all your online content, whether it's your website, blog, email, social media and all types of marketing communication (visiting cards, brochures, banners, TV Ads etc), so that your target audience can have the same experience, no matter where they go.

1) Logo

Undoubtedly a logo is the most memorable piece of a brand's image. If someone can't quite recall your brand name, they're likely to remember that visual sign associated with it. For example, when you think of Mercedes, can you see the steering wheel? If you hear Apple, does the image of an bitten Apple comes in your mind? What about Microsoft? We definitely associate Microsoft with a window sign ! These companies have spent a lot of time, energy and money building their brand image, and their logos go hand-in-hand with their vision of building a great brand. Logos gives an opportunity for customers to naturally associate products or services with any given brand. Some logos don't need eye-catching graphics to stand out. Brands like Amazon created logos with their names in distinctive fonts that forms a visual cue.

2) Colors

Branding is done well when seeing certain colors immediately calls to mind a particular brand – even when those brands' names are nowhere nearby. A good color scheme can go a long way. Let's talk about Coca Cola for example, when we talk about the red color which brand comes to your mind Coca Cola or McDonalds. Take Facebook for example. Regardless of updates to its newsfeed and small tweaks to the logo, that medium blue tone is instantly recognizable.   These brands have been seamlessly using the color tone which represents their brands across all their advertising and physical marketing channels.

3) Tone and Voice

Have you ever thought that your brand is not only visual but it also has a voice. Think about this; what does your brand sound like? Are you irreverent? Silly? Professional? Academic? All of the above? This may actually fluctuate somewhat between channels. Emails may be more formal, and social media may be more casual. That's totally fine! But there should still be a unifying factor; a blanket mission statement or mantra that all content adheres to. Bear in mind that at some stage, you're going to need to address a controversial or otherwise difficult issue. It's up to you to make sure you remain true to your mission statement, both when promoting the positive aspects of your brand and when responding to negativity. It's up to you to determine how to incorporate those viewpoints into your overall brand voice- and sometimes to turn down opportunities to jump into certain conversations for the sake of your brand.

4) Images

When you share an image, regardless of the platform you use, should take into account all of the above points we discussed. This means they should reflect the tone your brand has set out for itself, follow a color palette and include your brand's logo. It's simply not enough to randomly add images to your content and hope they look good. Instead, you should be methodical in your selection to guarantee that your visual identity is just as strong as your written one. Would cartoons or graphics suit your brand, or are you better off using high-quality photos? In the digital age, when consumers are facing a constant barrage of material, it's important to stand out for the right reasons, not for an inconsistent or poorly thought out image that takes away from your overall brand message.

5) Domain Name

Booking a domain name seems to be a easy task but its not. You'd be surprised how often domain name selection can go wrong. Your domain name should be well aligned with the brand itself, and it needs to be easy for your customers to find. Great domain names are spontaneous, they're short and they help your customer to get access to the information about you they're looking for immediately. For example, "verylongdomainnamesyoucannotremember.com", is very frustrating and tiring to type as a link or do a search in the search engines. What's more, that customer will probably have made a spelling error or two, sending them straight back to square one. So, make sure you spend a bit of time coming up with a domain that's easy to remember (and spell) to drive more traffic to your website.

6) Branded Links

Branded link? Now you might think why do I need a branded link when I already have a logo, website and a domain name but trust me you need it in this digital age. Branded link is a shortened URL built around a brand name (or products, services offered) that helps associate the brand with the links, content, and information they share online. Simply put, it's a shorter version of a URL that showcases your company name. Generic website links that are made up of a random string of numbers and letters, branded links reinforce brand awareness and increase trust.

They're completely customizable and have been shown to increase clickthrough rates by up to 43%. These links can also be used for tracking purpose it can be a good source of information for analytics purpose. Branded links provide a strong quality signal about the content you share,and aligning your content with your brand will establish authority in any industry. You can create your branded link / shortened links on https://bitly.com/ or https://goo.gl/

Recap

Brands today need to be extra careful when communicating their brand message. As consumers today are over bombarded with content which means getting consumers attention span is getting smaller and smaller and brands need to be cautious and creative to catch their attention.

Make sure to get right to the point without overly wordy text, include eye-catching images and if you're using a link, make sure it's a branded link that indicates where the user will go if they do indeed click on it. Taking some extra time to really concentrate on the quality of the material you're sending out will go a long way to make sure that potential customers have
meaningful interactions with it. Remember, in spite of all your best efforts as a company to shape your brand identity to fit a certain mold, you need to understand how your audience and customers perceive your brand will ultimately determine how successful your efforts are. At the end of the day, it's consumers that build brands- not companies.

Key Ingredients for Building a Great Brand

Branding to a lot of people not in the know, "branding" as a job profile can seem vague. It's such a generic term that, when you get down to it, can mean just about anything you choose it to mean. How do you quantify branding enough to fit it into a job description?

Just think about this:

Branding surrounds just about everything you do as a brand marketer, to some extent.

I am sharing with you a few explicit branding essentials for you to implement in the inbound marketing age.

1) Website

A brands website is one of the most important brand touch point for your customers. Like the way to keep your physical office neat, clean, well designed and maintained in the same way your website is like your virtual office and it should also be neat, clean, visually appealing and comfortable for the visitors to navigate. You also have to make sure that your site is simple to understand, your logo transitions seamlessly from one page to another and little details like the font and color palette remain constant. These design elements, however small they may seem, are an essential part of the brand building process.

2) Content Creation

If content is the King then contextual content is the Queen. Great content is how you exhibit the expertise your business has mastered over the years. Content can be in the form of a blogs, videos, whitepapers, ebooks, case studies, and much more. Your content allows your customers to get to know you more in depth. You should apply the 80:20 rule while working on what content you can share with your target audience.   Remember, 80% of the content should be user preferred content it should be about what your customers are more interested in, it can be an advice on an issue, latest news on industry updates, step by step guide to solve a particular problem or something your target audience will find interesting.

No matter whatever means you choose to present your content, there are a few things it needs to do: it should establish your brand identity, it should be of great value to your customers, and it should build up trust in your brand.

3) Social Media

A major difference that sets digital marketing apart from traditional marketing is the opportunity to strike a two way conversation with your target audience. A successful brand today behaves like a human it connects with its customers, chats with them on messages, answer their questions in real-time, help them resolve their queries, or just let them about the latest product development, some milestones achieved or just a normal good morning. This is what social media is all about for brands! It gives you an opportunity to communicate directly with your target audience and establish your brand as trustworthy in their minds, creating an impression that will define how they think of you for years to come. Also remember social media is a two sided sword, it managed well it can work wonders for your brand like never before and if not then it may also backfire and damage your brand image, so whatever you do on social media make sure it's a well thought of and a planned move.

Brand Value Proposition

Unlike in space where silence is everything on the other hand in the cyberspace it is just the opposite. In the social media age everyone is broadcasting information be it brands or individuals. It's very difficult to grab someone's attention towards what you want to say. To make yourself heard above other, you need to have the strongest and the clearest voice. Now this voice is your value proposition because this voice will make your brand unique and more qualified than your competition.

Your brand value proposition is the only thing that can provide you competitive advantage over others, and it is the most important takeaway for people while considering your brand.

It's very important that you do it right and your brand value proposition should be woven into all your marketing communication channels like your website, emails, social media, blogs, advertisements etc.

What is a Brand Value Proposition?

A brand value proposition is a commitment of value to be delivered to the customers. It's the main reason a prospect should buy from you, and not from your competitor. So what does one look like? A strong value proposition can be described as follows...

1) What You Do

Define exactly what your business does in very clear terms. For example, if you're a brand marketing company, your value proposition might be: "Our company does strategic brand development and marketing through digital media which helps increase brand awareness, build brand engagements, generate leads and drive traffic on your website."

2) How You Do It

Now let's describe exactly how you do what you do. Continuing on the example of a brand marketing company, you might write, "Our company uses deep industry knowledge and cutting-edge methodologies such as affiliates, influencers, bloggers, email, and social media marketing, combined with a team of digital marketing experts and state of the art analytics to ensure your business found online by your prospective customers."

3) How You Do It

Now let's describe exactly how you do what you do. Continuing on the example of a brand marketing company, you might write, "Our company uses deep industry knowledge and cutting-edge methodologies such as affiliates, influencers, bloggers, email, and social media marketing, combined with a team of digital marketing experts and state of the art analytics to ensure your business found online by your prospective customers."

2) Why you matter?

This is a very important question every brand must answer to know why they exist. Is there a specific problem there are trying to solve in the market place or they just exist like any other company. Tommorow if you are not in the business which you are right now, will it matter to anybody that you no more exist, will it be a great loss to the industry or not. So why your existence matter and what problem you are trying to solve is of ultimate importance.

4) For Whom You Do It

Brands today are more successful and effective once they establish a niche, and become an expert in it. Customers today don't have the problem of budgets or funds but the only problem they face is to identify which is the right company who understands their specific needs and challenges and is in a position to address and solve them.

Taking the same example of the brand marketing company, let's assume your niche is healthcare. You've handled dozens of healthcare clients including clinics, hospitals, diagnostic centers and pharmaceutical companies etc and helped them build up great brand presence and increased their online sales. So when a small clinic comes along and wants to hire your company, you know exactly where to start. When they tell you about their business and the challenges they face, you know what they need and how to help them. You know what their ultimate goals are, and how they can be achieved. But then another client comes along – this one a travel website. On the surface, they seem similar enough: you're promoting a product and trying to get customers to make an online purchase. So you take them on ... and it's a disaster. The way they do business is completely different. You try to get into the technical ins and outs of their company, but you don't really understand what issues they're dealing with. Or, worse yet, you think you do, but it's actually a very different situation. You try to approach them the same way you do with your healthcare clients and end up failing.

Every industry, target audience and location is different and your prospective customers want to know that you understand theirs. Rather than being a jack-of-all trades and master of none, it's better to find one industry to specialize in, and become as much an expert in it as your customers are. The better you know your niche, the better you'll be able to promote yourself within it.
It's very important to apply this to all your digital marketing tactics. You're more likely to find success by focusing on just one thing and doing it better than anyone else. Specialization is what the internet is all about. It's not a coincidence that businesses are reaping huge benefits from keyword optimization and social media marketing. So it's critical that you stand out from the crowd and create your own niche expertise.

4) What Makes You Different

Identify the "Secret Sauce" that makes all the difference in whatever you do. It can be a great customer service, great product design, excellent product performance, great job on the given assignment, have an emotional connect with your customers, a brand that cares not only for its customers but also for the environment and the society. So whatever it may be, just identify that secret sauce and include it in your companies mission statement and practice it no matter what.

How to Determine Your Value Proposition

Who is your customer?

Now.. how do you identify that "special sauce" factor? How do you figure out what to focus on when promoting your brand?

Here are a few things you need to do:

• Make sure you have a deep understanding of the customers you are targeting.

• Identify and understand their needs and goals.

• Position their brand as the best fit to meet the needs of the target customers

Let's go through a little exercise to determine a value proposition. We'll use a brand marketing company as an example again.

Who is your customer?

Prospective clients want to know that the company they hire for their brand promotion understands their business the same way they do. A real estate developer, for example, wants to know that the company he selects understands the process and nuances that their customers go through when selecting a builder. You need to know that homeowners are anxious about the credibility of the developer and his expertise in these kind of projects, customers will also consider the time commitment that a building project requires to complete. So be prepared to speak a real estate developers language to gain their trust—and their business.

What does your customer want?

Any prospective client would want their marketing agency to do one thing for them: improve their bottom line. But how will you do that? You need to show them using the metrics that they are most likely to care about when it comes to digital marketing:

• Increased traffic to their website.

• More high-quality leads from that traffic.

• Increased conversion of those leads.

• Overall business growth over time of your marketing endeavours with data driven evaluation and analytics.

If the niche you specialize in has other metrics that they're looking to move, it's important to be aware of what they are and how to move them. This is just one more way to show your prospects that you speak their language.

Nothing else matters if you can't convince your customers that you will do the best job than anyone else.

Anyone can say that they're the best but you can prove it with case studies and real-time data that shows your performance. By demonstrating a successful track record for your own agency, and the successes of your existing customers, you will have evidence that you can get the job done if not you then who else will get it done. Once you've answered all of these questions for your own business, you're ready to start crafting a brand that targets your ideal customers.

Buyer Persona Creation

Now just think about your ideal customer in a normal way; what do they do for a living , what are their interests, what they like and dislike and what kind of products or services they are looking for. To target them more effectively you need to know what kind of people your target customers are? To know all of that information about your ideal customer you need a buyer persona.

For example: you are a healthcare brand and your target customers are doctors, let's give it a name say "Dr.Mary" now What is her practice? what's her life like, how she must be spending her day? When she must be free? what kind of events she must be attending? What kind of friends she must be having? Which social media channels she must be most active? Now all this information will help you to give a name and face and also help you to understand your customers in more detail.

All your communications like blogs, social media, white papers and other inbound content should be written as if addressing this buyer persona. This makes it easier to target and connect with customers on a more personal, individual level, without having to tailor a different approach for every single customer. A buyer persona should include:

Demography

Let's understand some of the key demographics for your target market – e.g. gender, marital status, location, age range or income level – you will begin to get a sense of who your customers might be and narrow down their range of interests.

Job Level/Seniority

All the B2B marketers out there please remember even though you're selling to a business, you're still dealing with a person within that business. No matter how big the organization is, but the people working in those organizations are normal people like you and me who also have a Facebook account, who also go on Google to seek information and who is also watching videos on YouTube.

Now who are they in the company? What are their roles and responsibilities? What authority do they have in the decision-making process with regards to making this purchase? A CEO of a small business thinks and acts differently than the marketing manager at a mid-sized company or an MNC, and the same can be said for managers in enterprise organizations. In the same way, identifying a customer's job is important for B2C companies as well. A homemaker is looking for something different than a young salesperson straight out of college.

Typical Day

If you can piece together a customer's routine on a typical day, you'll understand many of the things that occupy their time, and what is and isn't important to them. If you can identify your ideal customer daily routine it can be the most crucial information because it will help you to understand what your customers actually care for.

It is advisable to align your value proposition with what their customers care about and figure out how to communicate that value proposition to the customer, then you're a branding rockstar.

Pain Points

Identify what yours ideal customers problems will be like? What keeps them up at night? What problems do they need the most help solving? If you can get a handle on that, then you'll be even better prepared to position yourself as the brand that will help them solve those problems, so that they can rest easy day and night.

Source of Information

How is the buyer researching their problem? Where do they get their news? What do they read? Do they consume blogs? White papers? Infographics? What social media do they use, and how do they use it? Once you know where the buyer is going for information, you can put your information there for them to find.

Objections

Let's be honest and real, objections will always be there. Even if you know that your company is the best one for the job, but the customer isn't convinced yet. Why not? Figure out the reasons why the buyer is still hesitant to make a purchase and why they might opt not to make the purchase from you. Ready yourself and your team with answers to these objections that will alleviate their prospects' concerns – communicated in a fashion that will appeal to the specific persona you've created.

Below are some common doubts which may arise in your minds about creating a buyers persona…

1. **Why do I need to make a buyer persona?** Because if you aren't clear on who you are marketing to and how you add value, you will fail.

2. **I have multiple products, where do I start**? Start by creating a buyer persona for your best product / service (e.g. highest profits, least hassle, multiple orders, quickest sale etc.).

3. **Is this applicable for B2B?** Of course! Think about the person who is making the buying decision in the company. What is their role, responsibilities etc. and how you can remove pain points and help them achieve their targets!

4. **Is this applicable to Affiliate Marketing or Network Marketing?** Of course! It doesn't matter if the products are not yours. You still need to be clear on who you are selling to and how you are adding value.

Chapter –4
Putting your Brand into Action

How to use Buyer Persona

Now since you have identified your buyer personas, use this information to communicate with them effectively through all your brand touch points:

• Develop content that can appeal to their needs, wants, interests and goals.

• Place content in the channels where prospective buyers are most likely see them.

• Develop highly targeted content that appeals to buyers' needs, goals, and interests.

• Since you already on which channels your buyers are most
active, place your content carefully on these channels so that they can see them.

• Grab their attention with highly informative and engaging content with high quality images, infographics, branded links and call to action.

• It will entice qualified leads with much higher ROI.

• Share customer insights across teams so that everyone knows about their target customers.

• Try to improve the quality of your persona base over a period of time so that it becomes more accurate.

• Knowing your buyers persona will help you design better products and services which will best suit their needs.

Now let's see how buyer persona can help you personalize your brand experience.

How to Build a Brand Experience Online

In the digital media, brands now have access to tons of customer data through various analytical tools available online. All social media channels have their own marketing tools which also provides a lot of valuable data to marketers so that they can create a segmented and personalized brand experience for them. If, for example, you have a range of products you offer on your website but 80% of your sales comes from 20% of the products, this show a lot about what kind of content you are showing your website visitors, what offers you are running and your advertisement is build around what products and services. It that's why very important to make sure that you not only provide lots of content but also contextual content. Providing content on a wide variety of different niche topics that apply to your industry gives you an upper hand over your competition to figure out what their potential customers are interested in and in what type of content they show more interest.

Let's say for example you are provider of a variety of CRM software ranging from HRM, CRM, Accouting etc so when a potential customer visits your website and is interested in the Accounting software and instead of signing up for the free software trial, the customer goes to the knowledge base and downloads the video on how the software can help to manage the business accounts now once the customer is in your funnel you should provide more and more valuable content on accounting so that you are able to nurture the customers interest in that product.

This is will increase their engagement the product and also the brand. And once you are able to target customers more effectively, they'll take more actions and will share more readily on their social networks which will build and enhance the brand experience

Great Brand = Great Content + Wow Experience

It's only a company's content that defines how their brand is perceived online. And when I talk about content its about everything be it your physical store, website, social media, sales person, customer care, advertisements etc... Now every piece of content you publish online or offline defines your brand. So, Great Content = Great Brand and Boring Content = Boring Brand so what are your building? Sometimes, what you choose not to publish says a lot more about your brand than what you do publish.

When in doubt about what content to post and what not to; go back to your brand value, brand promise, mission and vision statement it will help you to take the right decision.

Some important questions you need to ask yourself before developing your content strategy:

• Is this topic interesting to my buyer persona? If I was the buyer would I like and share this content?

• Does this content provide any value to my customer and address their pain points?

• What is the most preferred format in which my buyers would consume this content?

• Do they trust the way you're presenting your content, or are they unsure whether they should click on your links in the first place?

• What would be the best tone to publish this content? Like: funny, emotional, sad, happy, professional, serious etc.

• Last but very important, what is the purpose of sharing this content?

If you are able to answer honestly to all these question then and are fully convinced before sharing any content online then trust me there is nothing which can stop you achieving great success online.

Don't forget to ask these questions about every single piece of content you develop and share: social media updates, blog posts, links, ebooks, FAQs, videos, social media photos. Anything you publish under a particular brand contributes to the audience's overall view of that brand and will affect it either positively or negatively. Hence every piece of content before sharing should be carefully thought about.

Importance of Social Media

Social media presence is of ultimate importance when building a successful brand online. Brands today need multiple platforms to interact with their customers but this doesn't mean that all social media channel is right for your brand because different type of target customer's use different social media sites for different purpose.

Its impossible to maintain an effective presence on all social platforms simultaneously, but it's important to determine which ones will best help you reach your target persona, and focus your efforts on building up their brand and presence on those specific channels. I am sure you are familiar with all the social media websites but I am going to give you a quick rundown on how to use each of them for the best results.

1) Facebook

With over 1.2 billion user's worldwide and counting, having a Facebook Page is of outmost important and no brand in whatever business they are can afford to ignore this giant. Facebook is best for building engagement with your target persona with the help of videos, infographics, photos, links, and building community engagement. You can engage your target audience organically and also with facebook sponsored ads wherein Facebook will help you to reach your target buyer personas with help of its highly advanced and effective marketing tools. So keep a budget aside for Facebook marketing to get the best results out of this social platform.

2) Twitter

Twitter is a platform where brands can have casual communication with its target customers, share their view, updates and talk about things which matter the most to them and their customers, be it some news, some trending hashtag for some funny tweet by a know personality. Twitter as a platform is highly engaging and it keeps its users connected and engaged in real-time, with short bursts of information called "Tweets", in 280 characters or fewer with the latest update. This gives you a platform to communicate in an informal, personable way – even if that's not how your brand usually operates. Brands which really understand Twitter and are using it effectively and are the ones who are celebrating social media success with their customers.

Using the right "Hashtags" is a very useful tool for branding. Creating a hashtag specific to your brand, product or service allows you to group all of the related conversations about it together on a single, easy-to-find page. Make sure to spread the word about your brand by frequently tagging your tweets with it and encouraging your followers to do the same. Due to limited space make sure you use custom branded links as a call to action.

3) Instagram

A picture says a lot more than words and yes that's absolutely right with Instagram. On Instagram well placed images and videos can work wonders for any brand. Instagram supports branding creativity and can be useful in capture users' attention, connecting with them, and even encouraging them to post pictures of their own and tag your brand. And, like Twitter, it also uses hashtags to identify and group together content on a particular topic. With Instagram be as creative as you can with images, videos and infographics to build the best brand experience with your customers.

4) LinkedIn

LinkedIn is one of the important platforms for brands which are into the B2B business. If used wisely it can be a good platform to generate qualified leads and build connections. It helps brands to position and reinforce its thought leadership position in the industry.

Please note that LinkedIn is professional network and unlike Facebook, Twitter & Instagram you have to be extremely careful on what type of content you are sharing with your buyer personas. It's a platform where you can participate in relevant discussions, share your company's view on the topic and make a contribution. This will help foster long term relationships with other LinkedIn members and these efforts will pay off in the long run.

5) YouTube

The next big thing in digital marketing will be videos and it is the main reason behind the success of video content sharing platforms like YouTube. It is a great platform to share visual content in form of a video. Let me tell you it's also a social media site where you can build engagement with your target customers and strike a two way communication where you share the content and they can comment, like, share, download and do much more. YouTube's success can be achieved only through good original content based on the likes and interest of your audience. Brands now a days use Youtube for everything be it an interview, customer testimony, walkthrough video, product launch videos, product information videos, behind the scenes, glimpses into your company and much more which helps them to build a strong presence.

Identifying a Brands Voice

Brands not only have a logo, color or a website that identifies them but it also has a voice or tone that it applies to all their content – or communication – which helps their customers identify a brand's personality. Your voice or tone of communication makes an integral part of your website, blog, social media, emails and everything else between you and your customers. For building a successful brand presence online its very important that whatever tone you select to communicate it should be consistent to achieve great results.

You must be very well aware about the fine lines between being casual and serious, being helpful and intrusive, being educational or boring, as it will determine whether people find a brand appealing or abrasive and as a brand you should always try to strike the right balance.

Now how will you know when you've struck the right balance? Take your buyer persona, and mix their expectations with your "special sauce." Then, adjust over time based on feedback and results, just like any recipe from your kitchen. For example, Ford Motors uses multiple Twitter handles to communicate with different sets of buyers and also different Twitter handles for different countries. Some of their early customers right now are maybe in their 60's or 70s and some are just out of college teenagers/graduates/working professionals and they communicate in different tones familiar with their different buyer personas.

Lets take one more example, If you have seen Flipkart.com (One of the top e-commerce companies in India) has commercials which are aired on TV and on all digital media platforms, their tone of communication with the target audience is funny with school kids acting as matured mens and womens and talking in matured voice and people love their commercials eagerly wait for them to come.

On Flipkarts Facebook page, their tone is a combination of casual and playful which anyone would like. The voice of your brand should naturally adjust to suit the medium in which the content is being published, as well as to the people you are attracting to those particular media.

Presentation and Appearance

Why a grocer places food staples such as milk and grains at the back of the store? So that customers will have to pass by and view a myriad of other "excess" items before they get to the products which they need. On the other hand high margin desired items such as candies and snacks are placed in the checkout line for easy access while you wait for your billing.

Similarly, your website is their store, and your content is the inventory. It needs to be presented well for maximum impact.
Getting the right presentation and appearance for a brand's content from call-to-action buttons to ebooks – plays a significant role in determining a brand's success. Certain personas prefer text-heavy content, while others prefer images and visuals, and still others like shorter content that doesn't exceed five pages. These are the same considerations you should have when structuring a website around a brand.

Use the below tips while presenting content on the website and other digital platforms to support your brand marketing strategy:

Tip #1

Before publishing any content its highly recommended to do your research. Performing A/B testing to see how visitors will actually use the site and content, and make the changes accordingly. Ensure that the content and the links should flow organically form one point to the other.
Tip #2

It's not about what your customers want to buy but it's about what you want to sell. So plan the placement of the content and products on the website accordingly. If you place higher margin products or services than it will result in higher revenue for the business.

Tip #3

Always ensure that you place the right CTA (Call To Action) button in between the content to generate higher qualified leads and move the buyer a step further in the sales cycle.

Tip #4

Make sure that the content which you are sharing is of high value to your target customers.

Tip #5

Ensure that all your content is sharable so that customers who are viewing it can also share it with like minded people who would share it further and increase your brand awareness.

Tip #6

Keep your website clean and organized and your URL's simple so that it doesn't look messy and confusing which is also like by search engines.

Chapter – 5
Monitoring Your Brand

Brand Observation

The internet world is like the Wild Wild West you don't have any idea how far a content can reach, its beyond your imagination. When people are talking about your brand on multiple platforms other than your own page, they're mentioning you in their posts, in their conversations, blogging about you, making videos about you, they're mentioning their experience with you on their own Facebook pages and other social media channels. Not only that they are also discussing about your brand in various groups and communities on LinkedIn and Facebook and as a brand you need to keep a close eye on these activities

Honestly, some of this conversation may be good, and some of it may be bad for your brand and some of it may even be outright lies. But for better or for worse, it will live on the internet forever. As a brand what you can do, however, is to observe these conversation. Off-course, you can't snap every comment out there, but you can keep an eye on the important and bigger channels which may affect your brands reputation.

One of the best ways to keep a track of the conversations happening about your brand all over the internet is to create Google Alerts for your brand and keep watch on important keywords associated with it. Today there are also a lot of third party analytical tools which you can use to keep a close watch on all the activities pertaining to your brand. All the social media channels too have their own tool which constantly keeps you posted through notifications if someone mentions your name or tags you in their conversation or posts. Later, you can implement damage control when needed, or extend the reach of people's positive experience into your own channels.

Social Tracking

If you want to effectively monitor your brand in the digital world you need to have all types of analysis about your customer.

If you have a conversion or sale its very important to know where did this customer come from, Blog? Website? Social Media? Or Email Marketing? What type of content influenced the customer to buy from us? For how long the customer was in the funnel and how did it take to the conversion.

There are various third party software which provide indepth analysis on all of your brand activities online and what key activities are driving results and giving the best ROI.

How to do Social Tracking

Yes its true, tracking every mention of your brand online is a gigantic task and by just thinking about it can give you nightmares. And you would be right. As I mentioned already, it's literally impossible to cover everything being said about a brand. However, I also mentioned that there are tools to help you.

Google has made our jobs easier with their super gigantic servers and web crawlers, which make keeping tabs on your brand online much simpler, with tools like Google Alerts. Input terms you need to track that are important for brand management. These are the terms that encompass:

• Brand name.

• Names of Key employees, public facing employees, management teams and if possible brand ambassadors (if any).

• Product names, services and features

Amazing! So now you have good understanding on how, when, and where your brand is mentioned online.

Important Tip:

With Google Alerts you can also keep a close watch on competitor's activities too. Maybe you may get some key information about your competitor which can help you leverage your brand activity online.

Managing the Bad

You think of biggest and the most successful brand of today and do a Google search about them, you will still find bad reviews, comments and stories shared about them. It's never about having a bad comment or review but it's always about how you handle that comment defines your brands personality. And just like in life, in social media also there are three ways a brand can be mentioned: The Good, the Bad, and the Ugly and as a responsible brand you need to be prepared for all three. Keep the below points in mind while handling bad or ugly situation:

- Distinguish between crisis and normal bumps
- Make a response plan
- Assign teams to handle the situations

For example, a dissatisfied customer might go to customer service, a technical glitch will go to the IT department and legal problem will go to the legal team.

It's important to be highly responsive on these situations as it is critical for maintaining the good brand reputation you've built up over time. But the key is timeliness. Any crisis or PR disaster can be smoothed over, but the longer you wait to respond, the longer the negative press has a chance to spread, with nothing to quench the flames. They say there's no such thing as bad publicity, but some events can seriously, even permanently damage your reputation if not dealt with properly.

What happens if you ignore the grass in your garden, it will grow right under your feet.

It means you can buy time to handle the situation but you should not ignore the situation because if you do then it may sometime go out of control and may do a permanent damage to your brands reputation

Celebrating the Good

It's not always bad, offcourse good things too happen on the internet and the internet world is very neutral. It presents as many opportunities for good publicity as it does for, well, less-good publicity. Use the good stuff on the social media where someone left you a testimonial, a good rating or social mention which will help you build your brand reputation so don't miss these opportunities and whenever you get a chance make sure you celebrate it with your audience. Always look for opportunities to turn someone else's loss into your gain (tactfully, of course), and shine the spotlight on your marketing savvy.

For instance, when there was demonetization in India, PayTm used it as an opportunity to not only build their marketing campaigns around it but they also helped small retailers and normal people to do transactions with their PayTm wallet. It was a huge success and win-win situation for the brand, the people and the small businesses.

If your brand is a spa or a restaurant and you support the "Swach Bharat" campaign then once a month make your staff wear your brands T-shirt and start cleaning the locality where you are running the business it will show to people that you are a social brand and you care. Don't forget to click lots of selfies, photos and videos of smiling, blissful faces people who appreciate your efforts and make sure you post them on social media and gain leverage for your brand.

Chapter – 6
Measuring Your Brand

Measuring the ROI

Your Facebook likes on your page and posts, how much revenue does that translate to? Your Twitter followers and retweets, does that make the cash register ringing? When someone visits your website, reads your blog, and downloads your ebook, do you know if they ultimately bought what you are selling? And the answer to all of these questions is probably a big "NO".

If there is no proper tracking and analysis of your customers data then all this seems to look like isolated incidents which may be related, or they may not. There are lot of tools easily available which lets you see what happened from the first click at the top of the funnel to the "Buy Now" click at the bottom of the funnel, and everything in between. It tells you everything about how your marketing efforts are paying off.

When the management asks a brand manager or a prospective client asks a digital marketing agency "What's the return on investment for these branding efforts?" and you were unsure of the answer, or said something like, "To increase awareness," then you're not alone.

Awareness is just not enough. You may be aware of the Ferrari brand, but chances are you haven't bought one. So how valuable is that brand awareness to Ferrari or its marketing team? Zero. Awareness, unless followed at some point by consideration, intention, and purchase (the typical sales funnel model), is worthless.

It's important that you correlate the awareness you create to the purchases people make, to understand the ROI of your branding initiatives.

If you don't understand the ROI of your own branding initiatives, you'll never be able to demonstrate their value to executives and other teams at your company. It doesn't mean that every Facebook Like and Twitter retweets needs to translate into a sale in order to matter. A mass social reach means larger social buildup, which gets your content out there to the people who will eventually contribute to your bottom line. Additionally, maintaining an email list of evangelists – people who love your brand, will forward your content, but will never buy it – is equally valuable.

A very precise way of monitoring conversations it's essential that you look to your links. And if you want to analyze the source of any conversion, the best way to do it is through link tracking. Monitoring which platforms your customers are coming from is simple and free tools like www.bitly.com that track each click on your links, giving you accurate information about the source, time, location and much more. This will allow you to understand every aspect of your traffic so that you really know what people do on your site and how they got there in the first place.

Here are some specific metrics you can use to measure individual aspects of your branding efforts.

• Identify which keywords, short and/or long-tail, result in the most click throughs to your landing pages. If you're running paid campaigns, these are excellent venues to experiment with new brand elements, such as a new tagline, or a new value proposition, to see if it resonates and drives revenues

• For a blogs success see how many people are liking, commenting and social sharing your blog and keep creating more content around the likes of your audience.

• Tracking your email marketing campaign is very crucial as it will help to understand which type of emails have maximum forwards, open rate and click throughs so that you can effectively plan your future campaigns.

• Trying and testing multiple landing pages options helps you to see which pages are giving you the highest conversion at the best cost per click.

• Experiment with multiple links to see which links are working for your business and which are not.

• Find out the relationship between the increase in Facebook likes during a campaign and the sales during that period.

• See which type of content on social media generates the highest level engagement and try to make your future content strategy based on that analysis and also see if that engagement ever leads to a sale and if yes then at what percentage.

Conclusion

Everything you know about brands and brand management in the real world holds true in the inbound age. What's different is that now your brand extends far beyond the world over which agencies have traditionally had control. Before, when a customer had a complaint about your brand, only you, they, and perhaps a small circle of their friends and family knew about it. Now, anybody with an internet connection knows how to find – or memorialize – that complaint forever.

In the inbound age, there are so many moving pieces to managing a brand, from the website to the call center to the Facebook Page, to the LinkedIn group, to whatever that brings. As a result, you need to be more active, more vigilant, and more knowledgeable than ever to realize and prove maximum return on the investment of establishing a knockout brand.

Closed-loop marketing software, mixed with excellent branding created to drive the results you want, is the magic combination for a successful branding strategy.

For free tips on branding and marketing visit my website: www.chetanpillai.com and subscribe to my YouTube channel and please don't forget follow my page on Facebook, Twitter and Instagram.

Direct links to all my social media pages can be accessed through my website.

Branding Basics 2.0 is in the making and it will be launched soon…

This book will give you more in-depth view of your brand and also share with you the most advanced and proven techniques adopted by brands worldwide with case studies of modern and traditional brands.

www.ingramcontent.com/pod-product-compliance
Lightning Source LLC
Chambersburg PA
CBHW030518220526
45464CB00006B/2848